The Truth (& Myths) About
Weird Animals

by L. A. Peacock

illustrated by Jon Davis

Scholastic Inc.

To Joan Macri, who loves all animals, especially the weird ones
— With love, L.A.F.

Contents

How many kinds of bats are there?

More than a thousand. The United States has forty-five kinds of bats. They are **nocturnal** animals. Most bats hunt insects at night. Some eat fish or fruit. A few, such as vampire bats, drink blood.

TRUTH or MYTH?

Bats are related to birds.

MYTH! Bats are mammals. They have skeletons similar to humans'. They are born alive and feed milk to their young. Their bodies are covered with hair and fur.

BATS HAVE ARM, LEG, HAND, AND FEET BONES.

SKIN COVERS THEIR LONG ARMS TO FORM WINGS.

TRUTH or MYTH?

Bats are the only mammals that fly.

TRUTH! Bats can climb, hop, or swim, but they mostly fly. Some can fly as fast as thirty miles per hour.

What's the world's biggest bat?

The giant flying fox. It weighs about two pounds. From tip to tip, its wings can span six feet.

Where does it live?

The flying fox lives in treetops in the **tropics** and feeds on ripe, juicy fruit.

I DON'T THINK WE'RE ALONE!

What's the smallest bat?

The Kitti's hog-nosed bat. It's about the size of a bee. It's also the world's smallest mammal.

How many insects can some bats eat in an hour?

About a thousand.

How do bats find their way in the dark?

They use **echolocation** to find objects in the night. Bats make sounds through their noses and mouths that bounce off flying insects. The sounds reach the bats' ears as an echo.

THE ECHO TELLS THE BAT HOW FAR AWAY THE INSECT IS AND HOW BIG IT IS ...

... AND ITS SPEED AND DIRECTION.

TRUTH or MYTH?

Vampire bats suck blood with their razor-sharp fangs.
MYTH! Bats lick up blood with their tongues.

Why are bat bites dangerous for humans and most animals?

The bat can leave behind germs that are harmful. Dangerous infections, such as **rabies**, can cause death if untreated.

How do vampire bats feed off the blood of cows or horses?

The animals are always asleep when the bat bites. Chemicals in the bat's saliva numb the animal's skin. The animal doesn't feel the bite and doesn't wake up.

Why don't vampire bats bite dogs?

Dogs can hear the bat's high-pitched screeching sound. They wake up before the bat can attack.

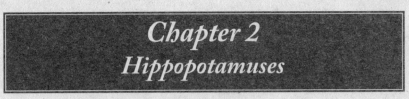

Chapter 2
Hippopotamuses

What's a close relative of the hippopotamus?

The pig. Its eyes, ears, and hooves are similar. Most hippos live in the rivers of sub-Saharan Africa.

How big is a baby hippo?

At birth, a hippo can weigh 110 pounds. Adults can weigh more than 7,000 pounds. The hippo is the second-largest land animal. Only elephants are bigger.

How big are hippos' heads?

About a third of their body size.

What's on top?

Their eyes, ears, and nostrils. Their position helps hippos to see, hear, and breathe while almost totally **submerged**. Hippos spend eighteen hours sleeping in the water and the other six hours eating.

When do they eat?

At night, hippos leave the water to graze on grasses near shore. They are nocturnal animals and can wander up to five miles to find food.

Why do hippos move so easily underwater?

Their webbed feet act as paddles in the water. Their feet also help them to spread their weight when they walk along the river bottom. Hippos can stay underwater for up to five minutes.

TRUTH or MYTH?

Hippos can't sweat to control their body temperature. **TRUTH!** The drops of liquid that come from their skin act as sunscreen, not to keep the hippos cool. That's why hippos spend all day in the water.

Why do birds sit on hippos and peck at their skin?

The birds eat **parasites** that live in the hippos' thick skin. Both benefit. The birds get fed, and the hippos get their backs scratched. It's a **symbiotic** relationship.

Are hippos dangerous?

Yes. They have a quick temper. Hippos can swim under boats and use their big heads to dump people into the water. Then they attack with their huge jaws. Hippos kill more people than any other wild animal in Africa.

What's their secret weapon?

The two knifelike teeth on their lower jaw. The teeth can grow as long as twelve inches.

Why do hippos fight each other?

Mostly over territory. They can battle for hours to the death.

What bird is known by the color of its feet?

The blue-footed booby. This wacky-looking bird lives in the Galápagos Islands and along the Mexican and South American Pacific coast.

Who named it?

The bird's name, booby, probably comes from the Spanish word *bobo*, meaning "stupid" or "dumb." Early Spanish explorers didn't think these strange birds were smart.

TRUTH or MYTH?

Blue-footed boobies live mainly on or over water.
TRUTH! They're marine birds. That's why they look so clumsy walking on land on their big blue feet.

Why are their feet blue?

The blue color comes from special **pigments** from their diet of fresh fish. When boobies don't eat for forty-eight hours, the brightness of their feet decreases.

Do the blue feet affect the male's success in finding a mate?

Yes. Female boobies are attracted to healthy, younger males with bright feet. The brightness of the feet decreases with age, so older boobies are often out of luck.

THESE BIRDS CAN WEIGH THREE POUNDS AND GROW TO THIRTY-FIVE INCHES LONG.

AND HAVE A FIVE-FOOT WING SPAN.

How often do they give birth?

Every eight to nine months. The female lays two or three eggs. The male and female take turns **incubating** the eggs. The chicks hatch after forty-one to forty-five days.

How do the babies get fed?

From the mouths of their mothers and fathers. The babies eat fish that are first eaten and spit back up, or **regurgitated**, by their parents.

When do males feel like dancing?

At mating time. They show off to attract females. They hop around from one blue foot to the other, holding one foot high to impress a future mate.

What else happens in this wild mating dance?

The male raises his wings and tail, while pointing his head and beak to the sky. The male whistles. If the female honks in reply, both raise their beaks and dance around together.

Chapter 4
Leeches

What are leeches?

They're legless, boneless, slimy animals that are related to worms. Some leeches have suckers at each end. Others have sharp teeth. Leeches can attach to the skin of humans and suck blood. When they're full, they drop off.

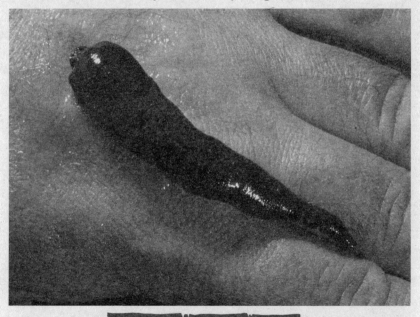

TRUTH or MYTH?

Most leeches attack humans.

MYTH! There are more than 600 species of leeches. Only a few feed on human blood.

Where are leeches found?

Almost any shallow, slow-moving freshwater makes a good home. Leeches are often found in jungles, marshes, and other wet areas around the world.

Why can't people feel a leech bite?

Because leeches inject chemicals that act as an **anesthetic** when they bite. This numbs the pain when the leech attaches itself.

How do people know they've been bitten?

A drop of blood appears on their skin.

What else is injected by the leech when it bites?

Another chemical that prevents the blood from clotting. This allows the leech to suck up the blood.

Should you squeeze the leech to get it off?

No, and don't try to burn it off or stab at it. This can cause the leech to empty its stomach into the bloodstream, along with dangerous germs.

How do you get rid of a leech?

Slide a fingernail or knife blade under it until it falls off.

Why did leeches almost disappear during the Middle Ages?

They were hunted so much because doctors needed them for bloodletting. Leeches were thought to cure illness by removing "bad blood" from the body. Sometimes a patient was covered with as many as fifty leeches.

Did bloodletting work?

No. Removing blood usually made the patients weaker. Sometimes it brought on their deaths. Bloodletting stopped when scientists discovered that germs, not bad blood, cause diseases.

When are leeches used today in medicine?

Sometimes during skin **grafting**, when skin is moved from one part of the body to another, leeches are used on the damaged skin. The blood doesn't clot and the new skin is more readily accepted.

Chapter 5
Kangaroos

What do kangaroos, koala bears, and wallabies have in common?

They are all **marsupials**. Most live in Australia and New Guinea.

What are marsupials?

These are animals that give birth to live young. When born, the tiny babies climb into their mother's pouch. They remain firmly attached, drinking their mother's milk, until they develop fully.

What is the biggest marsupial?

Australia's red kangaroo. Adults can weigh 200 pounds and grow to six feet long.

How long does the baby remain in its mother's pouch?

After about two months, the red kangaroo baby begins to spend time outside the pouch.

Why are kangaroo tails so strong and long?

Kangaroos need their tails for balance when they stand upright and while they jump.

How does a kangaroo use its tail in a fight?

It fights with its feet while balancing on its tail.

23

What do kangaroos do when they sense danger?

They thump their feet as a warning.

How high can a kangaroo jump?

In a single jump, a red kangaroo can leap six feet high and travel twenty-five feet.

HIGH JUMP
COMPETITION

What's their top speed?

Some kangaroos can reach speeds of thirty-five miles per hour.

Chapter 6
Sloths

Where do these strange mammals live?

Sloths live in the trees of South American rain forests. They are **arboreal** animals. They live in trees, sleeping as many as eighteen hours a day.

How do they hang on?

Sloths have long, sharp claws that they wrap around tree branches.

Are there different kinds of sloths?

Some sloths are "two-toed," while others are "three-toed." Both kinds have short claws on their front toes, and three claws on their back feet.

Do both kinds of sloth eat the same food?

Both species eat tree leaves. Sometimes the two-toed sloth includes insects and lizards in its diet.

TRUTH or MYTH?

Sloths are big eaters.

MYTH! They can go for days without eating. Once a week, the sloth goes to the ground to dig a hole to let out its waste.

How do they move on the ground?

Slowly. They are the world's slowest mammal. Their back feet are weak. Sloths use their arms to drag themselves along the forest floor.

What about in trees?

Sloths climb upside down through the tree branches. Sometimes they drop into the rivers and swamp waters below. They are good swimmers.

27

How often do sloths reproduce?

Sloth mothers have only one baby per year.

Why does their gray-brown fur look greenish?

Because of the algae that grow on the fur. The algae help sloths blend into the forest around them. The green color hides the sloths from **predators**.

What else grows on their fur?

Bacteria, which encourage beetles and moths to make their home in the sloth's fur coat.

SLOTHS GET THEIR LUNCH FROM LICKING THEIR OWN FUR.

Chapter 7
Hyenas

Where do hyenas make their home?

In the plains and forests of India and Africa.

How big do they get?

Some hyenas grow up to seven feet long, including the tail. They can weigh from 90 to 180 pounds.

What do hyenas look like?

Most people think they look like big dogs, but they're more closely related to cats. Both spotted and striped hyenas have coarse brown or black fur.

What parts do they eat?

Hyenas eat everything, including bones, hide, and teeth. What they can't digest, they spit back up in the form of **pellets**.

How have they adapted to their diet?

Hyenas have strong, muscular jaws. Their front teeth and premolars are also well suited for crushing bones and eating coarse food.

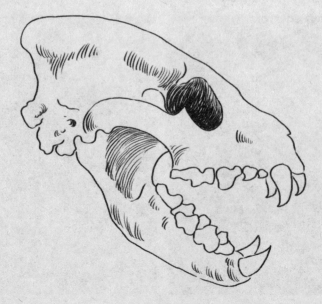

When does the spotted hyena make that funny humanlike laugh?

The hyena isn't laughing. It's showing fear and telling other hyenas in the pack to run because there's a predator nearby.

Who is their most common predator?

A male lion who doesn't have females to hunt for him. He'll hover around a pack of hyenas at a kill site. The lion will chase the hyenas away from the **carcass** and eat their meal.

UH-OH, HE'S BACK FOR DESSERT!

Why do hyenas have a hitch in their walk?

Their back legs are longer than their front legs.

How fast can they run?

Up to forty miles per hour. Speed helps them hunt for prey when no carcasses are found to scavenge.

Chapter 8
Platypuses

Where can you find these strange-looking creatures?

Only in Australia. The platypus lives in a billabong. That's what Australians call a watering hole of small streams and rivers.

Why does a platypus look so weird?

It looks like three animals put together. It has a duck's beak and webbed feet, an otter's silky body, and a beaver's tail. It can grow to twenty-four inches in length.

TRUTH or MYTH?

The platypus is a mammal.

TRUTH! Like all mammals, platypus babies feed on their mother's milk. But the platypus also lays eggs. It is a **monotreme**, the only mammal that lays eggs.

How many monotremes are there?

There are only five living species. One is the platypus. The others are species of echidna, another strange animal, living in Australia and New Guinea.

I THINK WE'RE RELATED.

What does the word *monotreme* mean?

"Single opening" in Greek. Unlike most mammals, monotremes use the same body part to poop, pee, and reproduce.

How do they give milk to their young?

Milk passes from the mother's skin into her fur. Baby monotremes then lick the milk off their mother's thick fur.

What does the platypus like to eat?

Shrimp, worms, fish eggs, and some plants.

THE PLATYPUS EATS 20 PERCENT OF ITS WEIGHT EACH DAY.

AND SPENDS TWELVE HOURS DAILY LOOKING FOR FOOD.

TRUTH or MYTH?

The platypus chews its food with sharp teeth.

MYTH! Adults are toothless. Playtpuses use their beaks to scoop up gravel to help chew their food.

How good a swimmer is the platypus?

Excellent. The platypus's body is well adapted for living in water. Its outer fur is waterproof. It propels itself through the water with its rudderlike tail and webbed feet.

What happens when you poke a platypus?

It growls. It will make louder noises when in **captivity**.

GRROWL

How does the platypus protect itself?

The male can shoot **venom** from a spur near its back leg. Only males can produce poison.

Is the venom dangerous?

It's not strong enough to kill a human, but can cause swelling and a lot of pain.

Chapter 9
Tarantulas

What's the world's largest, fattest, and hairiest spider?

The tarantula. There are more than 45,000 species of spiders, including 850 kinds of tarantulas. The Goliath is the biggest. This rain forest giant has a leg span of twelve inches. It feeds on small birds, lizards, frogs, and mice.

How long have tarantulas existed on Earth?

For more than 150 million years. Unlike dinosaurs, tarantulas are not **extinct**.

The thousands of spider species share these features:
a) two body segments
b) eight legs
c) antennae
d) produce silk
e) eight eyes
f) produce venom

The answers are *a*, *b*, and *d*. Not all spiders have eight eyes or are poisonous. Unlike insects, none have antennae.

Where do Goliath tarantulas make their home?

They dig holes, or **burrows**, in the rain forest floor.

TRUTH or MYTH?

The Goliaths are good housekeepers.

TRUTH! Their holes are clean and neat inside. When they need to go to the bathroom, they go outside.

FEMALE TARANTULAS ARE BIGGER THAN MALES AND LIVE LONGER.

SOME CAN LIVE TWENTY-FIVE YEARS.

How do tarantulas use the silk they produce from their bodies?

They don't weave webs. The silk is used to line their burrows. This keeps their homes moist and stops the burrows from collapsing.

Where is the silk made?

In glands inside the tarantula's **abdomen**. The silk threads come out of special openings in the tarantula's body.

Can tarantulas use their hair to protect themselves?

Yes. They can kick hairs off their back legs and aim them at predators. The hairs are covered with tiny **barbs**. These hairs can kill small animals and cause a bad skin rash in humans.

How else do tarantulas use their hairy legs?

The hairs act as sensors. They can detect **vibrations** from animals that are moving nearby.

How do tarantulas usually kill their prey?

They use their sharp fangs to inject venom into the animal. Tarantulas add chemicals to their food, so it turns to liquid. Then they suck up their meal.

TRUTH or MYTH?

Tarantulas are known for attacking people.

MYTH! They aren't killers. No one has ever died from a tarantula bite.

Do some tarantulas have fleas on their bodies?

Yes, some have small gray fleas crawling around their hairy legs. The fleas feed on the tarantulas' blood.

Chapter 10
Ostriches

What's the world's largest bird?

The ostrich, reaching up to nine feet in height. It's also the heaviest bird, weighing up to 290 pounds.

Are they the same as other birds?

Ostriches can't fly. They have only two toes on each foot. They use their powerful legs for running and for kicking at predators.

Where are ostriches found?

South of the Sahara, in the grasslands of southern Africa.

TRUTH or MYTH?

Ostriches prefer to live in groups.

TRUTH! They don't like to live on their own. A group of ostriches
is called a herd.

What do they feed on?

Insects, lizards, and plants. They swallow small stones to help
digest their food.

What makes the ostrich's legs
so powerful?

The location of the ankle. The joint halfway up the ostrich's leg
isn't the knee. It's the ankle. The rest of the foot is below that.

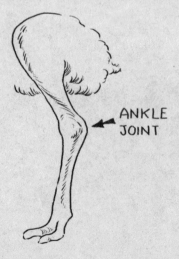

← ANKLE
JOINT

How fast can ostriches run?

Up to forty-five miles per hour. The ostrich is the fastest two-legged animal. It can keep its speed up for about thirty minutes. The cheetah is the only animal that can outrun it.

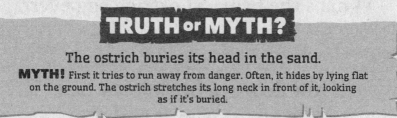

TRUTH or MYTH?

The ostrich buries its head in the sand.

MYTH! First it tries to run away from danger. Often, it hides by lying flat on the ground. The ostrich stretches its long neck in front of it, looking as if it's buried.

What if that doesn't work?

Then the ostrich will fight. It kicks out its powerful legs, attacking with the four-inch claws on each foot.

How big is an egg laid by an ostrich?

About six inches in diameter. It's the largest egg laid by a land animal.

What's the heaviest ostrich egg ever?

The one laid by an ostrich in Sweden in 2008. The egg weighed five pounds.

How do ostriches know when to go to sleep at night?

The herd leader yawns first. Then the others in the group yawn, one after the other.

Chapter 11
Lizards

What lizard can walk on water?

The little basilisk lizard. When frightened, it drops into the water from its treetop home. It stands upright and dashes across the water's surface on its back legs. That's why it's sometimes nicknamed the Jesus lizard.

Why doesn't it sink?

The basilisk's extra-large feet have wide soles. The flaps of skin on each toe also help it stand on the water.

How fast can the basilisk run on water?

It can sprint up to twenty steps a second. At four inches from head to tail, it's the largest animal able to run on water.

WHEN IT LOSES SPEED THE BASILISK SINKS.

IT CAN STAY UNDERWATER UP TO THIRTY MINUTES.

Where does the basilisk make its home?

Close to water, in the rain forests of South and Central America.

Where did it get its name?

From a **mythical** Greek monster who was half rooster and half snake. As the myth goes, one look from the monster could turn a person to stone.

Besides running away, how do other lizards hide from predators?

Most hide by staying still and trying not to be noticed. Some are colored like leaves or bark. Others, such as geckos, look like rocks on the desert floor.

What about chameleons?

The green-and-brown patterns of their skins blend in with the trees around them. They can also flatten their bodies to hide behind branches.

TRUTH or MYTH?

Some chameleons can change color.

TRUTH! Special cells in their skin contain pigments. The brain sends signals to the skin cells, telling which colors to show so the chameleon can hide.

What lizard is just as strange as the basilisk?

The Australian frilled lizard. When frightened, it rises on its back legs and displays a wide flap of skin around its neck and hisses loudly.

How does it do this?

Rods of **cartilage** in the lizard's skin flaps keep its collar stiff and upright. Usually, the "frill" is kept folded flat.

How big can the frill get?

The collar can expand up to four times the width of the lizard's body.

Chapter 12
Giant Anteaters

What are the furry creatures with bushy tails that you see hanging around termite mounds?

They're probably anteaters. If they live in the grasslands and forests of Central and South America, they're the really big ones—the giant anteaters.

How big do these animals get?

They can weigh up to ninety pounds. Some grow to four feet in length, or seven feet if you add the tail.

How do giant anteaters spend their time?

Wandering around, looking for their next meal. They dine on small insects, usually ants and termites.

Do they eat a lot?

Up to 30,000 insects in a single day.

Why is the giant anteater so good at insect hunting?

It has a long nose and a strong sense of smell. Its tongue is more than two feet long, well adapted for reaching into the small holes where insects live.

TRUTH or MYTH?

Anteaters use their sharp eyesight to look for food.

MYTH! They have poor eyesight. They depend on their sense of smell to find food.

How do they use their big, bushy tails?

They stand up on their back legs and lift their big tails. Then they spread out their tails, like umbrellas, to protect them from the hot sun.

51

How do anteaters get around?

They walk around on the **knuckles** of their front feet. They do this to keep their long claws out of the way.

Why are their claws so sharp?

For ripping through the rocklike termite nests to get to their next meal.

Chapter 13
Walruses

What keeps walruses warm in their icy Arctic home?

Like their seal cousins, walruses have a thick layer of fat, called **blubber**, under their skin. The blubber also stores extra food.

How big can they get?

Walruses can weigh up to 3,700 pounds, making them one of the world's biggest animals. Some are eleven feet long. That's bigger than most cars. Their tusks can grow up to three feet long.

The walrus's tusks are actually its upper canine teeth.

TRUTH! Like elephant tusks, the tusks of the walrus are made of ivory. This makes the walrus a valuable target for **poachers**.

PEOPLE MAKE CARVINGS FROM WALRUS TUSKS.

THIS KIND OF CARVING IS CALLED SCRIMSHAW.

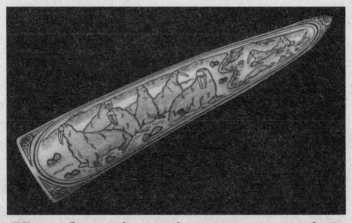

How does the walrus use its tusks?

Mostly to rake the ocean floor in search of food, especially shellfish. Some walruses eat more than 5,000 clams a day. Their diet also includes shrimp, crabs, octopuses, and mussels.

How strong are walrus tusks?

Strong enough to break through eight inches of ice. Walruses can use their tusks as ice picks to pull themselves out of the water.

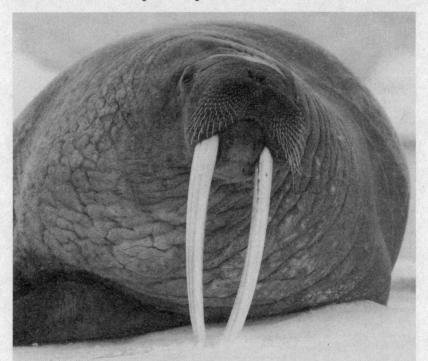

How much time do walruses spend in the water?

About two-thirds of their lives. Walruses have four flat flippers that make them good swimmers. They can hold their breath underwater for more than twenty-five minutes.

What happens when they get hot?

Walruses turn pink, just like people do.

Why do both male and female walruses have mustaches?

This row of long, coarse hairs on the snout is sensitive. The walrus uses its whiskers to search for food on the ocean floor.

TRUTH or MYTH?

The walrus's mating call sounds like a bell ringing.

TRUTH! The male makes a bell-like whistle to get the attention of a female. If she responds to his love song, they rub whiskers and then jump into the water together.

How often do walrus cows have babies?

A female walrus has one calf every other year.

FEMALE WALRUSES STAY IN THE SAME HERD AS THEIR MOTHERS.

MALES LEAVE AND JOIN A HERD OF BULLS.

Chapter 14
Puffer Fish

What happens when the puffer fish is attacked?

It inflates itself with water or air, so that its bigger size will scare away predators.

Is there a problem with this?

The ballooned size slows down the puffer fish. It just floats around, sometimes upside down, hoping that its attacker will leave it alone.

Does the puffer fish stay inflated for a long time?

Only until it's safe. Then the puffer releases the water or air, like a balloon deflating, and swims away.

What else can puffers do to hide from predators?

Some species change color, like chameleons, to blend in with their surroundings.

TRUTH or MYTH?

The puffer fish has four teeth.

TRUTH! The teeth are **fused** together, so they look like a small beak.

How do puffers use their teeth?

To crush the shells of crustaceans and mollusks, their natural prey.

Why are puffers different from most fish?

They don't have scales, and they can blink their eyes.

How big can they grow?

As big as twenty-four inches long, though some are as small as an inch.

Why aren't puffer fish on a restaurant menu?

They're extremely poisonous and can cause death when eaten.

How does the puffer fish cause death?

When the puffer is swallowed or eaten, its poison causes its victim to suffocate to death. The victim's **diaphragm** muscle is paralyzed, so the victim can't breathe.

How is the venom produced?

By bacteria in the puffer's **intestinal tract**.

Where is the puffer considered to be a special delicacy?

In Japan, Korea, and China. Specially trained cooks there know which parts of the puffer are safe to eat.

Chapter 15
Rhinoceroses

Where does the rhinoceros make its home?

There are five species. Three live in Asia. Black and white rhinos, the other two species, live on the grassy plains of southern Africa. They can live side by side because they eat different food.

How big are rhinos?

Only the elephant and the hippopotamus are bigger than the white rhino. The black rhino is smaller.

How fast can they run?

Fast, considering their weight. They can reach speeds of twenty-five miles per hour when charging a predator. That's the same speed as an Olympic sprinter.

BLACK RHINOS CAN WEIGH 3,000 POUNDS...

...AND GROW TO SIX FEET IN HEIGHT!

YOUR WEIRD ANIMALS I.Q.

Rhinos like to cover themselves in mud to

a) keep bugs away
b) hide from predators
c) cool themselves
d) protect their skin from the sun

The answers are *a*, *c*, and *d*. Rhinos can't sweat, so rolling in wet mud stops them from overheating.

TRUTH or MYTH?

A group of rhinos is called a posse.

MYTH! It's called a crash. A group of turkeys is called a posse.

When is a rhino fully grown?

At about seven years old. Rhinos can live to more than forty years of age.

What does the name rhinoceros mean?

It's made of two Greek words meaning "nose" and "horn."

TRUTH or MYTH?

The horn is part of the black rhino's skull.

MYTH! The horn sits on top of the nose. It's not part of the skull. The black rhino has two horns. The larger, front horn is used for digging for plants and water.

What is the horn made of?

Keratin, the same material that human hair and nails are made of. The rhino's horn can reach nineteen to fifty-three inches in length.

What animals are threats to rhinos?

Lion and hyena packs, which hunt young calves. If these predators come too close, the mother rhino will charge, thrusting her sharp front horn at the attacker.

Who are the rhino's most dangerous enemy?

Humans. Most rhinos are killed by poachers for their horns.

Why are the horns so valuable?

Some cultures, such as the Chinese, believe that the horns have magical healing powers. They pay a lot for rhino horns. An ounce of rhino horn is worth about the same as an ounce of gold.

Chapter 16
Naked Mole Rats

Is this weird animal a mole or a rat?

It's neither. The naked mole rat is actually a small mammal. But it does look like a hairless, wrinkly little mouse with buck teeth.

Where do they live?

Mostly in burrows underground in dry areas of eastern Africa.

How do naked mole rats spend most of their time?

Digging mazelike tunnels with their beaver teeth.

Don't they swallow a lot of dirt when they dig?

No. Their big teeth protect the mouth, which is kept closed when they dig.

How do they dig their tunnels?

The naked mole rats line up, one digger behind the other. They toss the dirt behind them. Each moves the dirt along like a bucket brigade.

Don't their teeth ever wear down?

No. Their teeth never stop growing, so they can dig all their lives.

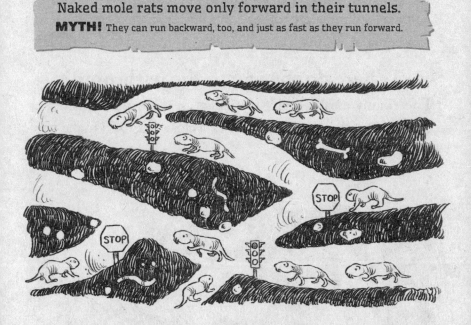

Why are naked mole rats like bees and ants?

They are organized in a **colony**. Like some insects, each member of the naked mole rat colony has a specific job. They are soldiers, housekeepers, workers, or breeders.

Do they have a queen who produces the young?

Yes. Like bees, when a new queen emerges, her body gets longer.

How big can their underground homes get?

Some naked mole rat colonies build tunnels that can cover an area equal to twenty football fields.

Where do they go to the bathroom?

The colony creates toilet chambers in their mazes. When a chamber is full, the naked mole rats close it up and make new ones.

How long have cockroaches been around?

For at least 280 million years. There are about 5,000 species worldwide.

Where did the American cockroach come from?

Africa. It's about one to two inches long. Its cousin in the tropics can grow up to four inches.

TRUTH or MYTH?

The cockroach's skeleton is on the outside of its body.

TRUTH! This kind of skeleton is called an **exoskeleton**. It protects the internal organs.

What does a cockroach look like?

It has a flat, oval-shaped brown or black body. The head has a pair of antennae. Only the male has two wings.

What do cockroaches like to eat?

Anything people eat, they'll eat.

Where do they like to live?

In dark, warm, and humid places, especially in kitchens close to their next meal.

How smart are cockroaches?

Smart enough to be trained to run complicated mazes. After five tries, they are able to find the correct pathway to home, each time faster than the previous one.

How fast can they run?

They can race across the kitchen floor at 3.5 miles per hour. Considering their size, that's like a human running at 190 miles per hour.

What do cockroaches use to detect movement?

Tiny hairs on their stomach pick up small vibrations in the air. Hairs on their legs also alert them to danger.

COCKROACH EYES HAVE 2,000 SEPARATE LENSES.

BUT THEY'RE COLOR-BLIND.

How do cockroaches get around?

They're excellent climbers and runners. Tiny claws on their feet help them grip any surface.

> COCKROACHES ARE GOOD AT GETTING INTO TINY PLACES.

> YOUNG ONES CAN FIT INTO CRACKS AS THIN AS A PIN.

> PUSH! YOU'RE ALMOST THROUGH!

Are they harmful to humans?

Cockroaches spread disease. And their dead bodies and waste can give off a bad smell.

What's the world's largest rodent?

The huge capybara, found in the Amazon rain forest. Some adults have been known to reach 200 pounds. Females are usually heavier than males.

Where does the capybara spend most of its time?

In the water, swimming. That's why it's known as a water hog.

Where do rodents get their name?

From the Lain word *rodere*, which means "to gnaw." All rodents, including squirrels, rats, and capybaras, use their long front teeth to bite and chew on food.

TRUTH or MYTH?

The capybara has four long front teeth.

TRUTH! These teeth never stop growing and always stay sharp.

THE SMALLEST RODENT IS ABOUT 1-5 INCHES LONG.

THE CAPYBARA GROWS UP TO 4-5 FEET LONG.

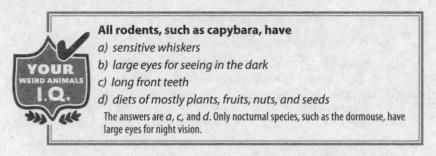

How often do capybaras reproduce?

They usually have one litter a year, producing four or five babies. A house mouse has up to 100 babies in about ten litters a year.

What's the life span of a capybara?

Near villages, they typically live eight to ten years. In the wild, they live fewer than four years.

CAPYBARAS ARE THE FAVORITE FOOD OF JAGUARS, OCELOTS, PUMAS...

...AND ANACONDAS!

Chapter 19
Penguins

How many kinds of penguins are there?

There are seventeen species. All have plump bodies with short legs, webbed feet, and flipper-like wings.

TRUTH or MYTH?

Penguins are found only in cold climates.

MYTH! They can live in the frigid waters around Antarctica all the way to the warm Galápagos Islands near the equator.

Can penguins fly?

No, but they can move like **torpedoes** in the water. They are fast swimmers, traveling up to eighteen miles per hour.

How do penguins walk on land?

They're clumsy and move slowly. To speed up on snow and ice, they often toboggan on their bellies to conserve energy. Some can jump up to six feet in the air.

LOOK AT THAT SHOW-OFF!

TRUTH or MYTH?

Penguins live near the seashore.

MYTH! Not all do. Each year, Adélie penguins leave their sea homes and march miles inland to their nesting site. They lay eggs and then return to the sea.

How do they find their way to their breeding colonies?

They **navigate** by means of the sun. They return to the same mates and nest sites each year.

TRUTH or MYTH?

Penguins sing to one another.
TRUTH! Some penguins sing to attract a mate.

Which is the largest penguin?

Emperor penguins. They can reach forty-five inches in height.

What does the male do after the female lays an egg?

The male emperor penguin takes over while the female goes to sea for food. He tucks the egg on top of his feet. A loose fold of his warm skin incubates the egg.

THE MALE PENGUIN INCUBATES THE EGG FOR ABOUT TWO MONTHS.

HE CAN LOSE UP TO 45 PERCENT OF HIS BODY FAT DURING THIS TIME.

How do penguin parents identify their offspring?

Each penguin chick has a unique call. Parents will feed only their own young. Once the chick is identified, the parent regurgitates food into its mouth.

When do baby penguins go off on their own?

First, they have to lose their soft baby feathers, which aren't waterproof. It takes up to thirteen months for protective feathers to grow in. Only then are the young chicks ready to swim and find their own food.

Chapter 20
Meerkats

Where do these weird creatures live?

Meerkats are cat-sized mammals that live in the dry, desert regions of southern Africa.

Are meerkats related to cats?

No, even though the word *meerkat* means "lake cat" in the South African Dutch language. And they don't live anywhere near lakes.

TRUTH or MYTH?

Meerkats live in well-organized groups called gangs.

TRUTH! Gangs of up to forty meerkats do everything together—watch for danger, search for food, and raise their young.

What helps the meerkat stand upright?

Its long tail acts as a third leg. This is important because many meerkats spend their days on **sentry** duty.

THE MEERKAT'S BODY IS ABOUT TWELVE INCHES LONG.

ITS TAIL ADDS ANOTHER SEVEN INCHES.

Why do they look like they're wearing sunglasses?

Meerkats have dark rings around their eyes, which help protect them from the hot desert sun.

Where do meerkats spend the night?

In the safety of their burrows in the soft desert sand. They can dig out their body weight in sand in a few seconds.

Why are meerkats so good at digging?

The long claws on their front feet are excellent **excavating** tools. Meerkats are also able to shut their ears while they dig, to keep the sand out.

How else do they use their claws?

For finding insects, spiders, and roots to eat.

How do meerkats build their burrows?

They take over burrows made by other animals or they dig their own. There can be two or three levels of tunnels six feet below the surface, with fifteen different entrances. If a deadly snake enters one tunnel, the meerkats can make a quick escape through another hole.

How does a female meerkat choose a mate?

She starts a courtship dance. The female picks out a male, jumping and making purring sounds. Then she chooses a mate. After ten weeks of **pregnancy**, she gives birth to three or four pups.

TRUTH or MYTH?

All adult meerkats reproduce.

MYTH! Only some do. The other adults help take care of the young, especially when the moms are away hunting for food.

How do the others help?

By babysitting. They keep meerkat pups warm and safe by standing guard against enemies.

Chapter 21
Turtles

What are the only reptiles with hard, protective shells?

Turtles, including their cousins, the tortoises.

Where are turtles found?

In mostly warm, hot climates. There are between 250 and 300 different species.

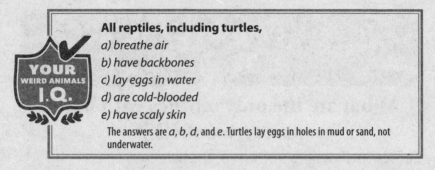
How are tortoises different from turtles?

Turtles live mostly in the water, while tortoises live on dry land. As swimmers, turtles have flipperlike limbs. The land-dwelling tortoise has legs that are short and thick.

TURTLES THAT LIVE IN PONDS AND RIVERS ARE KNOWN AS TERRAPINS.

Why are turtle and tortoise skeletons so unusual?

The shell is actually a part of the skeleton. Their ribs are fused to the upper shell. Turtles have flat shells. Tortoises have high-domed shells that protect them. Predators can't get their jaws around the dome.

Do tortoises and turtles have sharp teeth?

No, they haven't got any teeth. They use their horny beaks to cut and chew their food.

How does a baby turtle break out of its egg?

It uses its "egg tooth" to crack the shell. It's not really a tooth but a small spike near the tip of its beak.

What determines the gender of newly hatched Hermann tortoises?

The temperature on the ground. If the temperature is 86°F or higher, the young will be born female. If lower than 82°F, they'll all be males.

Where do the world's biggest tortoises live?

On the Galápagos Islands, off the coast of Ecuador.

Who was the last known giant tortoise from Galápagos's Pinta Island?

Lonesome George. George died of a heart attack on June 24, 2012, at about 100 years of age. He was the world's rarest creature.

Chapter 22
Manatees

Which large mammals spend all their lives in the warm water of the coasts and rivers of the southeastern United States?

The Florida, or West Indian, manatee. This gentle giant has a flat tail but no hind legs. Its front legs act as paddles.

PEOPLE CALL MANATEES "SEA COWS" BECAUSE THEY EAT UNDERWATER GRASSES.

BUT MANATEES ARE MORE RELATED TO ELEPHANTS.

How fast can manatees swim?

These slow-moving creatures look like small submarines. They glide through the water at two to six miles per hour.

How long can a manatee stay underwater?

For about fifteen minutes. Then it comes to the surface. The manatee sticks its tiny nostrils into the air to breathe. The rest of its body stays submerged.

LOOK AT THIS BIG FELLOW!

What helps the manatee to sink?

Its bones are heavy and dense. Also, it has long lungs that run along the back of its spine. The lungs keep the manatee afloat. When the manatee dives, it squeezes its lung muscles and expels air. The manatee rises when its lungs fill up with air again.

TRUTH or MYTH?

The manatee eats only plants.

TRUTH! It's an **herbivore**, and the only marine mammal that's a total vegetarian. It spends about eight hours a day just eating.

How much can a manatee eat?

About 9 percent of its body weight each day. Since an average Florida manatee can weigh 3,500 pounds, that's a lot of vegetation.

How does a manatee find its food?

It uses the short, stiff hairs on its lips and snout. When these whiskerlike hairs brush against plants, the manatee senses its next meal.

What do manatees do after every meal?

They clean their teeth. They roll small rocks inside their mouths to remove grass and dirt from their back teeth. Sometimes, manatees use an anchor rope as dental floss to get rid of stuck food.

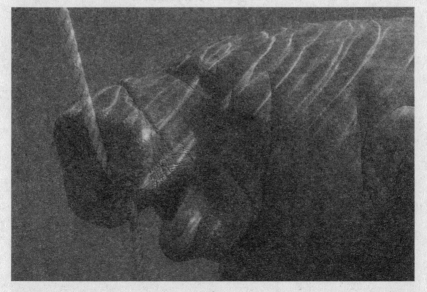

Are manatees endangered?

Yes. Over the years, they have been hunted illegally. Their **habitats** are often destroyed when people build homes close to the water. In Florida, about a quarter of all manatees are killed by motorboat propellers.

What do legends about mermaids have to do with manatees?

Sailors long ago claimed to see beautiful creatures, half fish and half woman, resting on rocks and singing. The sailors probably saw the floppy tails of manatees and heard their high-pitched sounds.

Which famous explorer reported seeing mermaids?

Columbus wrote in 1493 that his crew had seen three mermaids.

CAPTAIN, MERMAIDS AHEAD!

Glossary

abdomen—the part of the body below the chest that contains the stomach

anesthetic—a substance that makes a living thing unable to feel pain

arboreal—living in trees

barb—the point of an arrow or hook that points backward

blubber—the layer of fat around the body of a sea animal

burrow—a tunnel in the ground

captivity—the state of being kept in a closed space against your will

carcass—the dead body of an animal

cartilage—a very strong but bendable material found in some parts of the body

colony—a group of animals or plants that live together

diaphragm—the layer of muscles, between the lungs and the stomach, that controls breathing

echolocation—the use of sound waves and echoes to detect the distant location of objects

excavate—to make a hole in the ground by digging

exoskeleton—the hard outer body of some animals that protects the organs inside

extinct—no longer existing

fused—joined together

grafting—moving skin or bone from one part of the body to another part that has been damaged

habitat—a place where a plant or animal naturally lives or grows

herbivore—an animal that eats only plants

incubating—keeping eggs warm until they hatch

intestinal tract—the long tube leading down from the stomach, where food is digested and waste is carried out of the body

keratin—the substance that forms hair, horns, hooves, and feathers

knuckle—a joint in the fingers

marsupial—an animal that carries its young in a pocket of skin called a pouch

monotreme—an animal that lays eggs but also gives milk to its babies

mound—a small hill or pile of earth or stones

mythical—something imaginary and existing only in ancient stories

navigate—to find your position and the direction you need to go

nocturnal—active mainly during the night

parasite—an animal or plant that lives on another animal or plant and gets its food from it

pellet—a small hard ball of a substance that was previously soft

pigment—a natural substance that gives skin, leaves, etc., a particular color

poacher—a person who illegally hunts birds, animals, and fish on somebody else's property

predator—an animal that lives by killing and eating other animals

pregnancy—the time when a baby is developing inside the body of a woman or a female animal

rabies—a disease that can cause death in humans when infected animals bite them

regurgitate—to bring food that has been swallowed back up into the mouth again

scavenger—an animal that searches for dead animals to eat

sentry—guarding or protecting something

submerged—under the surface of water or other liquid

symbiotic—a relationship between two living creatures in which each benefits

torpedo—a weapon shaped like a tube that is shot underwater to hit a ship or submarine

tropics—the hottest part of the world

venom—a poisonous liquid produced by some spiders, snakes, etc.

vibration—a continuous, shaking movement or feeling